Mapping in the Modern World

MAPPING IN A DIGITAL WORLD

James Bow

Crabtree Publishing Company
www.crabtreebooks.com

Crabtree Publishing Company
www.crabtreebooks.com
1-800-387-7650

Published in Canada
616 Welland Ave.
St. Catharines, ON
L2M 5V6

Published in the United States
PMB 59051
350 Fifth Ave. 59th Floor
New York, NY 10118

Published in 2017 by CRABTREE PUBLISHING COMPANY

Author: James Bow

Managing Editor: Tim Cooke

Designer: Melissa Roskell

Cover Design: Katherine Berti

Picture Manager: Sophie Mortimer

Design Manager: Keith Davis

Editorial Director: Lindsey Lowe, Kathy Middleton

Editor: Janine Deschenes

Children's Publisher: Anne O'Daly

Proofreader: Ellen Rodger

Production coordinator and Prepress technician: Ken Wright

Print coordinator: Margaret Amy Salter

Produced by Brown Bear Books for
Crabtree Publishing Company

Photo credits
Photographs (t=top, b=bottom, l=left, r=right, c=center)

Front Cover: Wikimedia Commons: inset second from left, bkgd; All other images from Shutterstock

Interior: Alamy: Rosalrene Betancourt 6 22, Focus Technology 15, Jeff Greenberg 19, Picture Library 17; ESRI: 23; GeoSmart: Luigi Cappel 29c; Diansheng Guo/jack Grieve, Aston University/Andrea Nini, University of Manchester: 6; Google Inc.: 25, 27; Aaron Koblin: 10; NASA: 12, 13, 29t; NOAA: 7; NREL: 28; (c) OpenStreetMap contributors: 5; (c) Juha Oksanen, 2014, based on public Sports Tracker workouts, contains data from the National Land Survey of Finland's Topographic Database 7/2012, more information HYPERLINK "http://http://carde.fgi.fi/supra/english.html" http://http://carde.fgi.fi/supra/english.html: 4; Ordnance Survey: 1, 14, 29b; Shutterstock: Dennizn 26, M-SUV 24; SPL: Pasquale Sorrentino 21; United States Air Force: 16; United States Census Map: 9; USGS: 18; Fernanda Viegas & Martin Wattenberg: 11; U.S. Government Accountability Office: 20; World Mapper: 8.
All other photos, artwork and maps, Brown Bear Books.

Brown Bear Books has made every attempt to contact the copyright holder. If you have any information please contact licensing@brownbearbooks.co.uk

Library and Archives Canada Cataloguing in Publication

Bow, James, 1972-, author
Mapping in a digital world / James Bow.

(Mapping in the modern world)
Includes index.
Issued in print and electronic formats.
ISBN 978-0-7787-3223-5 (hardcover).--
ISBN 978-0-7787-3241-9 (softcover).--
ISBN 978-1-4271-1884-4 (HTML)

1. Cartography--Technological innovations--Juvenile literature. 2. Cartography--Computer programs--Juvenile literature. 3. Digital mapping--Juvenile literature. 4. Cartography--Data processing--Juvenile literature. I. Title.

GA102.4 E4 G46 2017 j526.0285 C2016-907124-3
C2016-907125-1

Library of Congress Cataloging-in-Publication Data

CIP available at the Library of Congress

Printed in Canada/052017/TL20170327

Contents

GATHERING DATA

Digital technology enables **cartographers** to gather huge amounts of data and to display it in different ways for use by governments, businesses, and individuals.

As technology develops, cartographers use the latest advancements to create innovative maps. Cartographers were among the first to develop ways of representing a spherical globe on a flat surface. They began to make maps on computers soon after the first computers appeared. From the 1980s, cartographers began to make maps that existed only in digital form and were stored in computers. In 1989, the English computer scientist Timothy Berners-Lee figured out a way to let computers share documents, leading to the development of the World Wide Web (www). Cartographers were quick to use the new technology to develop the maps you use today.

This map of Helsinki in Finland uses data from mobile sports apps to show routes for runners (blue), walkers (green), and cyclists (red). Mixed colors show where routes are shared by users. Gathering such information would not have been possible before the invention of the Internet.

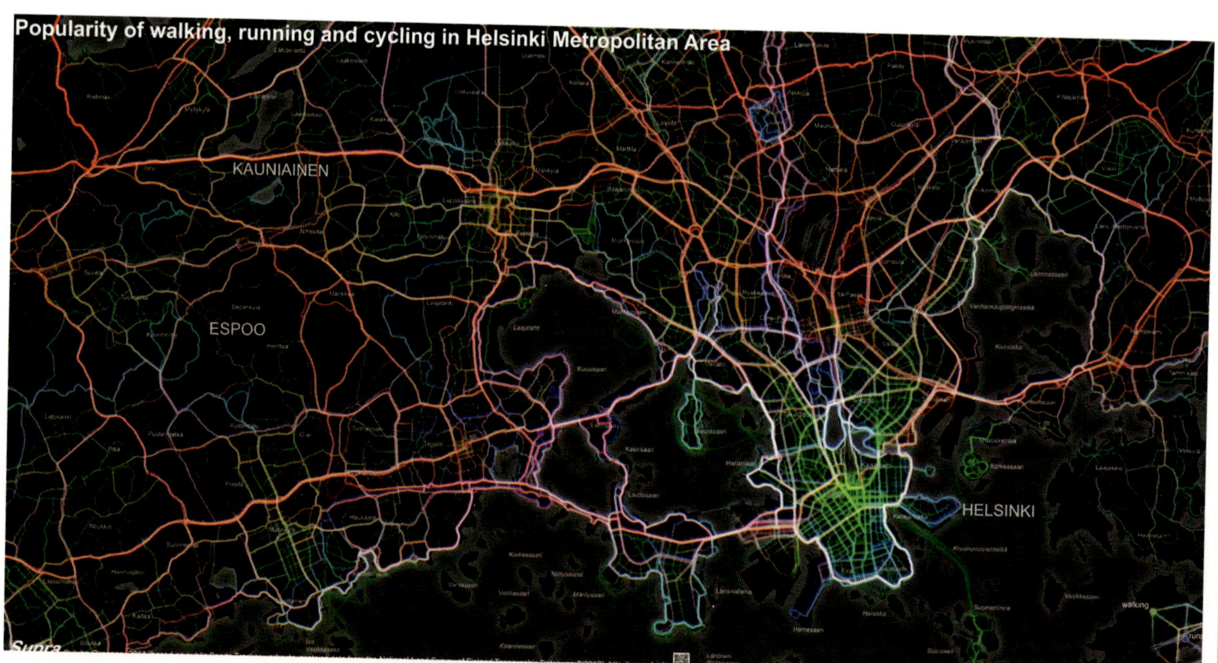

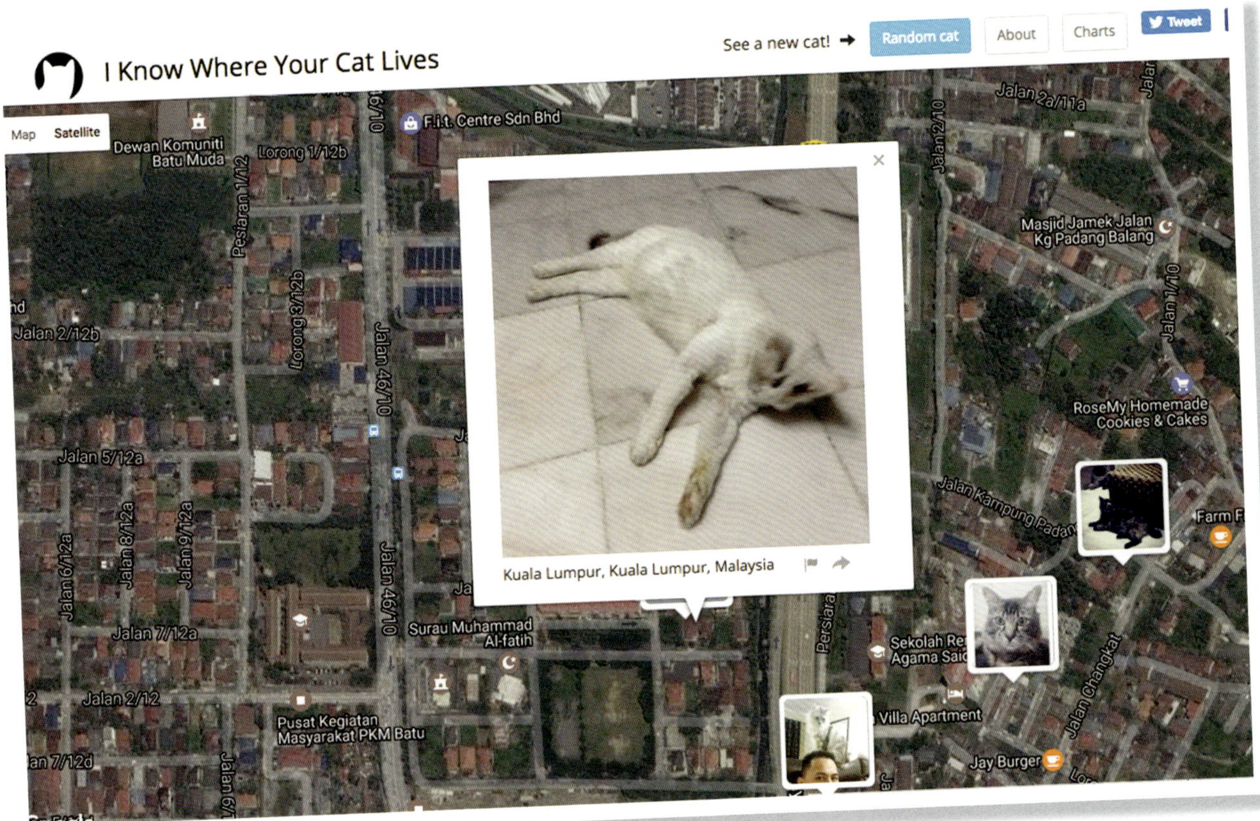

This map shows cats living in part of Kuala Lumpur, Singapore. Owen Mundy created the map, which covers the whole world, using pictures of people's cats that are freely available on the Internet.

New Formats

Digital computer technology allowed cartographers to create maps in new formats. These formats included interactive maps where users could select different options for display, or maps that could be updated in real time. Just as importantly, digital technology also gave cartographers new ways to access information to use in maps, and new ways to store and process it. For example, a digital media artist named Owen Mundy searches Internet sites for publicly posted images tagged with the word "cat." He has plotted the locations of more than a million pet cats on a world map. Mundy calls his map "I Know Where your Cat Lives." He wants the map to demonstrate the capacity of the Internet to gather and share any type of information.

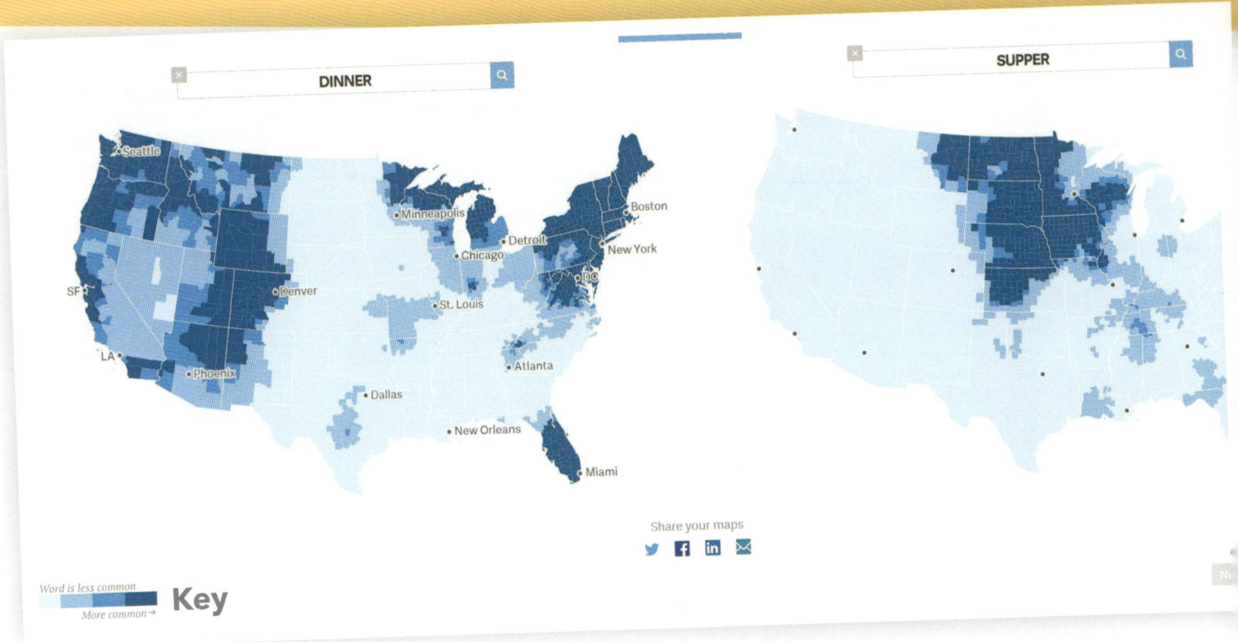

The Great American Word Mapper uses Twitter to map the use of language. These maps show where people in the United States call their evening meal "dinner" (left) and "supper " (right).

Digital maps can display a huge variety of data drawn from different sources. In addition to geographical data, such as the shape of mountains or the routes of rivers and roads, they may include information about the population in an area, where different types of vegetation can be found, or how far the average person lives from a fast-food restaurant. They can also depict **abstract** information such as how people use words in different ways.

Before the Internet existed, such information often took a long time to collect and sort into a format that could be used on maps. Maps usually relied on official figures, such as those collected in the national census. A census is a government survey of everyone in a country. It records where they live, and information such as their ethnicity, age, job, and religion.

In the Real World

Maps and the Internet

Gathering information from the Internet does not always give accurate results. People who mask their Internet Protocol (IP) address can only be traced to a whole country, not to the neighborhood where they live. The Internet allocates this incomplete data to a location in the middle of whichever country the IP address is located. Users with masked IP addresses are therefore not included in local data.

Breakthroughs

Information from Users

The Internet allows cartographers to react to input from map users. Google uses user feedback to correct mistakes on its maps. In the United States, the National Oceanic and Atmospheric Administration (NOAA) uses data from **amateur meteorologists** to add to its own weather reports to generate maps. Allowing users to add and adjust data is like adding thousands of researchers to a mapping project.

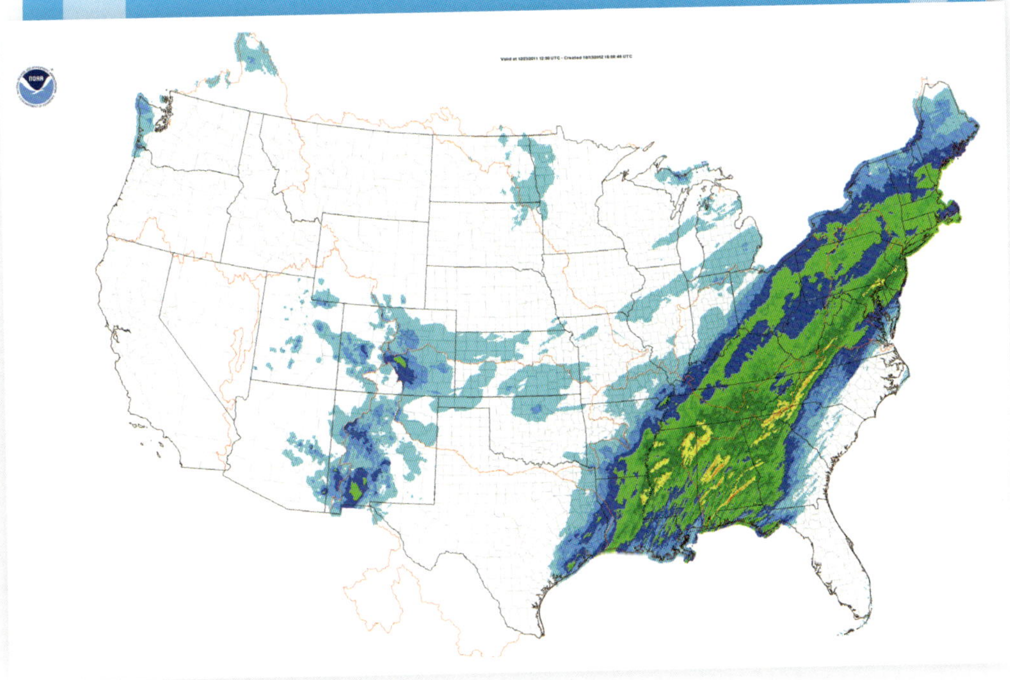

NOAA bases maps such as this chart of U.S. rainfall on both its weather stations and input from amateur weather watchers. The areas of heaviest rain are colored yellow and green.

The Canadian census is held every five years and the United States census is held every 10 years. Censuses provide useful information, but a several year gap between censuses means information isn't up-to-date.

Unfiltered Data

Today, cartographers use the Internet to gather sets of data that are not filtered by any kind of official organization. Data on the Internet does not only come from sources such as the census.

In the Real World

Displaying Data

Digital cartographers use various ways to display information, including traditional methods such as color keys and symbols. Often, maps use different colors, symbols, and shades to represent information. A key explains what each color, shade, or symbol represents. Symbols can also be used on their own. They are signs that carry information such as the population of a city, or perhaps the location of a celebrity home in Hollywood. Some symbols are standard, such as a wavy blue line for a river, but others are made up by the cartographer. A more unusual type of digital map is a **cartogram**. These maps convey information by distorting the shape of places. In the map below, Japan is unusually big, showing that its science funding is growing rapidly. Africa spends little on scientific research, so it is tiny.

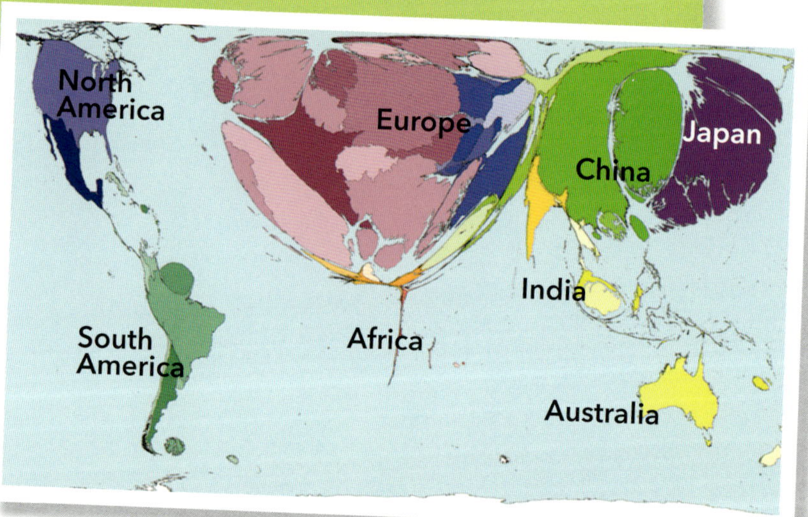

This cartogram distorts countries to look bigger or smaller depending on how much money they spend on science research.

Digital artists and cartographers use computer programs to gather information from social media sites such as Facebook or Instagram. These sites provide personal data about people's movements, their ethnicity or religion, and almost anything a person might post online as either text or images.

Most portable computers, smartphones, and tablets have **location services**. These work with **Global Positioning Systems** (GPS) to map the device's position on Earth. Any data gathered from these devices is tagged with the user's location,

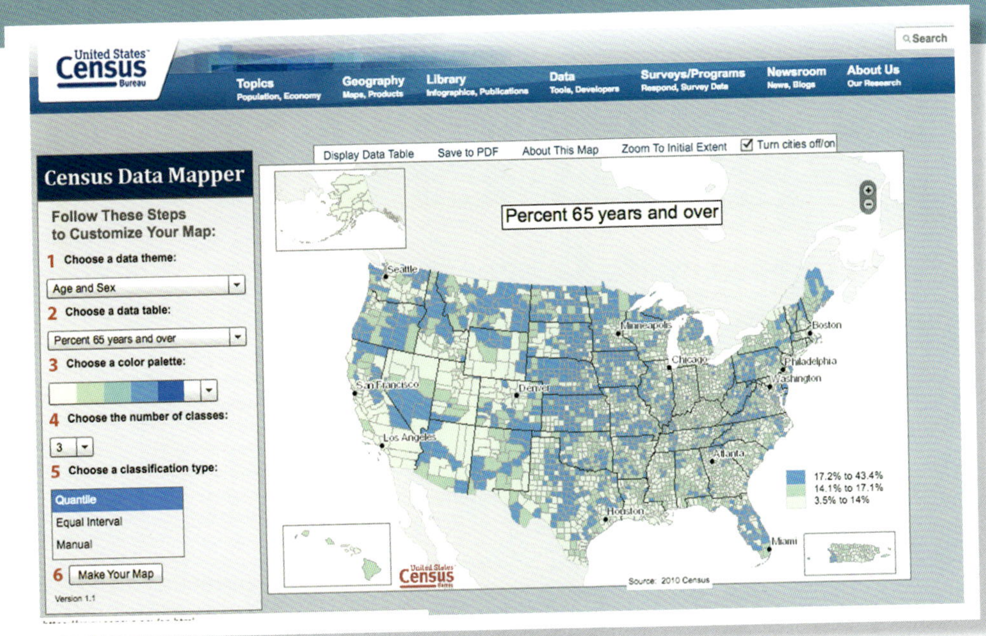

so a cartographer can easily place it on a map. Sometimes data collection from mobile devices happens without people realizing—although most cartographers who gather information from the Web **anonymize** it before they use it.

Users can select data to generate their own national or local maps on the U.S. Census website. This map shows the share of the population over 65 years old in each county.

A Huge Map

Social media users reveal information about themselves online, such as their religious faith, how much they earn, what schools they went or go to, and what languages they speak. When this data is tagged with their location, it is easy to turn into maps. Governments, researchers, and activist groups use this data to identify places where special help is needed to deal with social and environmental problems. For example, if many social media users in a place earn a low income, governments might spend more on social assistance there.

The Internet has made maps faster and easier to create. In many ways, the Web has become one huge map. It shows us everything we ever wanted to know about ourselves and the world—and even some things we might prefer not to reveal about ourselves.

Did You Know?

Some people are concerned that gathering data to create digital maps is an invasion of people's rights to keep details of their lives private. Other people argue that Internet data sets are so large, it is virtually impossible to find facts about individuals.

MAPPING CHANGES

Digital maps have made it easier to map important changes on Earth, from human activity to environmental impact. Cartographers can even create moving maps.

We usually think of maps as being static images printed on paper. However, the world is constantly changing. Some cartographers have begun using computers and the Internet to create video maps that show the world in motion. To show motion on a map, a cartographer layers video footage on top of a regular map. This mapping technique has been used to make maps of airplanes in flight over the United States. It is also used for mapping world weather systems. Being able to see movement clearly helps to highlight how a system behaves.

This is an image taken from a video map by Aaron Koblin. It shows aircraft routes over the United States. Whiter lines show the busiest routes at the time of filming.

In the Real World

Mapping the Wind

In 2012 two scientists—Fernanda Bertini Viégas from Brazil and Martin Wattenberg from the United States—created flow maps of the winds over the United States. They used the **database** of the U.S. National Weather Forecast, which is updated every hour, to make an animated map of the changing winds. Viégas and Wattenberg wanted to draw attention to the wind's potential to generate electricity by using wind farms.

This image from Viégas and Wattenberg's map shows the winds on January 10, 2017. The cartographers use thicker lines to indicate the winds that blow quickest.

Video Maps

Video maps sometimes show real-time information, such as traffic flow in a city. Other video maps show events that have already happened. Cartographers use computer programs to redraw the map information to produce a sequence over a period of time. This sequence is then run together as a movie. The technique is similar to that used in digital **animation**.

Photographing Earth

Digital technology has made it easier to map change. In the past, this was only possible if they mapped the same area at different times and then compared the maps. This was slow and difficult. Satellite photography has made the job quicker. Satellites constantly photograph the surface of Earth. They take photographs of the same areas each time they fly over them, and produce sequences of images showing how the same region changes over time.

Over the last 40 years, space satellites have taken millions of images using both visible light and **infrared**. Infrared light reveals features hidden by vegetation or even beneath the ground. The collection of images are a record of recent change on Earth. Mapping changes helps experts understand and predict weather patterns. For example, satellite maps of changing **ocean currents** and temperature help experts predict changes to the weather.

Did You Know?

Military forces study satellite images for signs of change on enemy bases. These changes might indicate that a country is building weapons such as missiles.

This map shows the course of Hurricane Matthew in early October 2016. The white clouds indicate strength of rainfall.

In the Real World

Mapping Hurricanes

Satellite data is used to predict the paths of hurricanes. Scientists compile data in computer **models** that map a hurricane's likely path. This makes it possible to evacuate areas that might be affected. Hurricanes are unpredictable, however. They can change course suddenly and might impact areas miles from their predicted course.

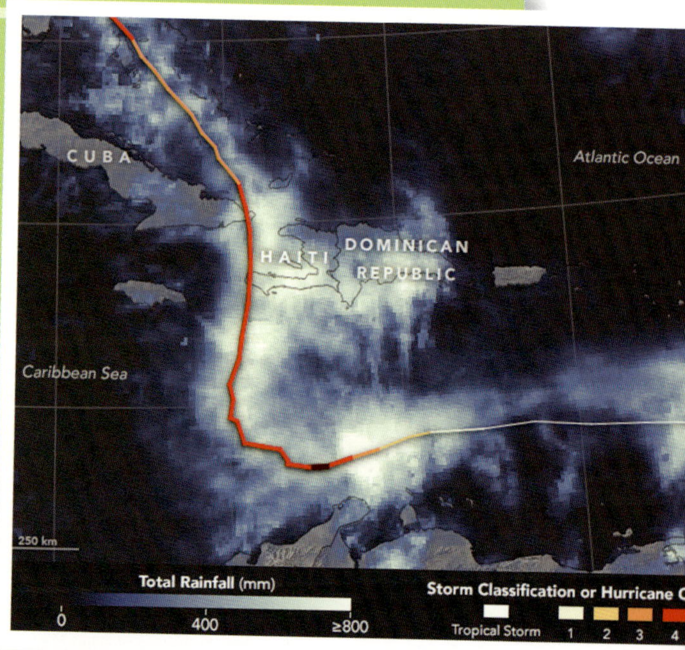

In the Real World

Building a Mosaic of Earth

The Landsat space satellite orbits Earth in a pattern that allows it to photograph the whole surface of the planet every 16 days. The images it takes are not always used exactly as they appear. Separate, detailed images are put together to form a **mosaic** of an area. Computers adjust the image to give a single viewpoint. This allows experts to put together the images where Earth's features are most clearly visible.

This Landsat image shows clouds along the course of the Mania River in Madagascar where it meets the sea.

The El Nino and La Nina weather events are caused by unusually warm or cold currents in the ocean. They disturb normal weather patterns across the Pacific Ocean from the United States to Australia. Other weather satellites monitor cloud formations, allowing experts to predict storms or hurricanes. These mapping technologies have made weather forecasting more reliable. They may also save lives by giving people time to evacuate from areas at risk from extreme weather.

Environmental Change

Maps of change help experts understand possible threats to the environment. Images of the shrinking **ice cap** in the Arctic Ocean or **deforestation** in the Amazon highlight the effects of global **climate change**. Cartographers who create maps showing such changes are part of a growing movement striving to understand how Earth works–in order to better preserve it.

VIRTUAL MAPS

Digital cartography has influenced the development of video games, which are often based on maps. Equally, technology developed for games influences modern cartography.

Since the early 1970s, video-game designers have developed computer programs to generate maps of the **fictional** places in video games. Many adventure games involve a quest or journey, so it is important for the player to know where his or her character is in the **virtual** world.

Since the 1980s, the mapping technology used in video games has grown more realistic. Many games now allow players to create their own worlds.

This 3-D map of the mountainous region of Snowdonia in Wales is part of a map of Great Britain created in 2013 using the Minecraft video game.

Breakthroughs

Computer-Aided Design

Computer-Aided Design (CAD) is a way of mapping objects in three dimensions. Designers use CAD to create accurate computer models of anything, from small objects to whole buildings. CAD uses math to create a virtual world where lines and shapes can be drawn so precisely that they are used to produce plans for solid objects. The programs allow users to turn an object to see it from all sides. CAD programs use the same data as mapmakers or modelers. One of the early uses of CAD was to produce highly accurate 3-D maps.

An architect uses CAD to design part of a bridge. The first CAD programs appeared in the 1960s, but modern CAD programs are far more advanced.

World of Minecraft

Minecraft is a video game in which players can use cubic blocks to construct **customized** 3-D worlds. Some players have also started to use Minecraft technology to make accurate maps of the real world. Individuals have made many 3-D maps of cities or regions, but official organizations have also produced Minecraft maps on a more ambitious scale. In 2013, the British Ordnance Survey–the official government mapping unit in Britain–created a Minecraft map of Britain. In 2014, the Danish government fed **topographic** information into a computer to create a Minecraft model of Denmark. The finished map used four trillion individual Minecraft blocks. Kids across Canada are also building a Minecraft map to mark the country's 150th birthday in July 2017.

Breakthroughs

The World in Detail

One challenge of mapping with computers is that the real world is full of curves and shades but computers are better at drawing straight lines. In the past, it was difficult to create 3-D maps with computers. If the maps were made larger, the lines looked blocky and unreal. In 1980, Loren Carpenter, a computer scientist at Boeing, figured out how to generate computer landscapes using **fractals**. Fractals mathematically divide a shape into smaller and smaller triangles that computers can use to model a realistic landscape using straight lines. These maps can be rotated or blown up to any scale.

A U.S. Air Force pilot flies an F-16 simulator during his training. The realistic landscape is created by digital mapping.

Simulated Landscapes

There are other ways that the technology used to map virtual worlds is becoming more involved in the real world. **Simulation** games such as Flight Simulator or Train Simulator allow players to re-create an accurate experience of landing a jet at real airports, such as O'Hare in Chicago, or driving high-speed trains across Europe. The games use satellite photographs and real-world mapping information to create realistic 3-D maps of the landscape. Some of the maps are so accurate that the U.S. military uses them to train pilots how to fly fighter planes. The landscape is projected on a screen that wraps around a flight simulator.

Advances in Printing

Another development that may change the role of virtual mapping in cartography is the development of 3-D printing. On flat maps, cartographers indicate **relief** by using shading or **contour lines**. Printing in 3-D allows cartographers to print a virtual map in relief to show its hills and valleys. This gives physical existence to a world that only previously existed on a flat screen. Normal 3-D printing is slow and expensive, but some cartographers are experimenting with 3-D maps built from precisely cut sheets of paper that are glued together to form a whole landscape. These 3-D maps are far cheaper to produce than other 3-D printing, even if they are large.

A user plays Pokémon GO on a smartphone. The game brings together virtual mapping with the users' movements in the real world.

In the Real World

Real-Life Video Games

The close link between real and virtual maps has created its own type of games. Geocaching is a game where players look for locations using map coordinates as part of a treasure hunt. The game Pokémon GO incorporates fantasy creatures with real-world maps. Players use the maps to hunt for rare virtual creatures using their smartphone to guide them. However, the game was criticized for leading people onto private property, into sensitive locations such as churches, or to dangerous places such as clifftops or railroad lines.

GIS SYSTEMS

Computer programs called Geographic Information Systems (GIS) allow cartographers to store and sort huge amounts of information to display on maps.

The Internet offers cartographers more access to information about the world than ever before. That means they can produce more specialized maps for users. Miners can study maps of an area's **geology** to know where best to dig or drill for minerals or fossil fuels. Activists trying to reduce environmental damage can create maps of plant life, soil conditions, and topography, or the physical features in an area. City planners might use maps of traffic patterns, water drainage, and air and soil quality to decide where it is best for homes to be built.

Collecting the Data

While maps have become more flexible, cartographers now often have to collect and sort huge amounts of data to create a map. The amount of data on the Internet is too big for traditional methods of research and mapping.

This map of the Eastern coastline of the United States uses GIS to map the makeup of the seabed as gravel (red), sand (yellow), and mud (green).

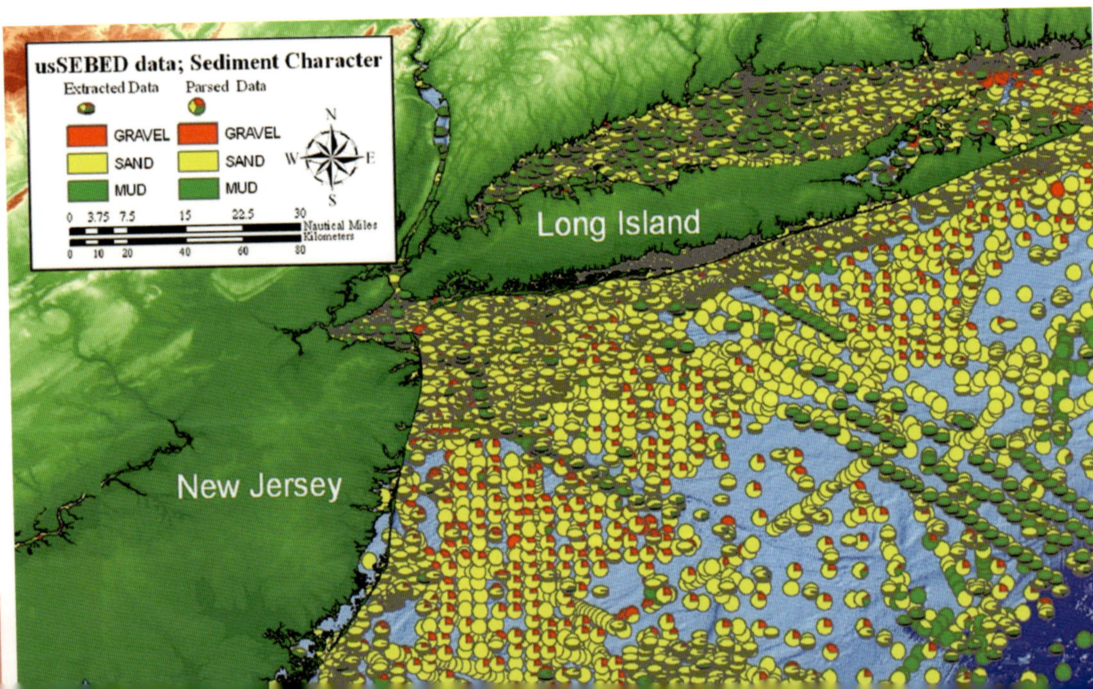

GIS allows city planners to customize maps. For example, a map might only show buildings of a certain age so that they can be checked by building inspectors.

Before digital technology was invented, cartographers had to analyze statistics from books or tables and plot them on a map using a color key or symbols. Today, cartographers use computer programs with GIS that can generate maps from millions of pieces of data.

Specialized Programs

The first GIS was developed in the 1960s. They became common in the 1980s. These specialized computer programs are designed to convert data into a form that can be displayed on a map.

Breakthroughs

GIS Display

GIS can combine digital maps drawn using two different methods: raster and vector. On raster maps, each **pixel** of the display contains a piece of information, such as a color or part of a road. If the maps are enlarged, the details lose definition, causing it to pixillate, or become blurry. Vector maps log geographical information as a series of points and lines. The maps can be enlarged or minimized without losing definition. Each point can have information assigned to it that cannot be seen, but that can be used by GIS. A user can therefore choose what details the map should hide or display.

In the Real World

Issues of Accuracy

GIS systems are capable of producing such detailed maps that they appear to be absolutely accurate. This is not always the case, however. A GIS map can only be as accurate as the data it is based on. Some data only exists for larger areas, such as counties or states, so data for smaller areas sometimes has to be estimated based on the data for larger areas. There is also the possibility that data can be entered incorrectly into a computer, or that it is not up to date. Users of maps produced by GIS should still remember that GIS maps can be as unreliable as any other forms of maps.

A GIS works by creating a huge database. It includes a wide range of information from different sources. This data may come from other maps, which can be scanned into the GIS and converted into a digital image. Data can also come from satellite images, which are already digitized. Tables of statistics can also be entered into the system.

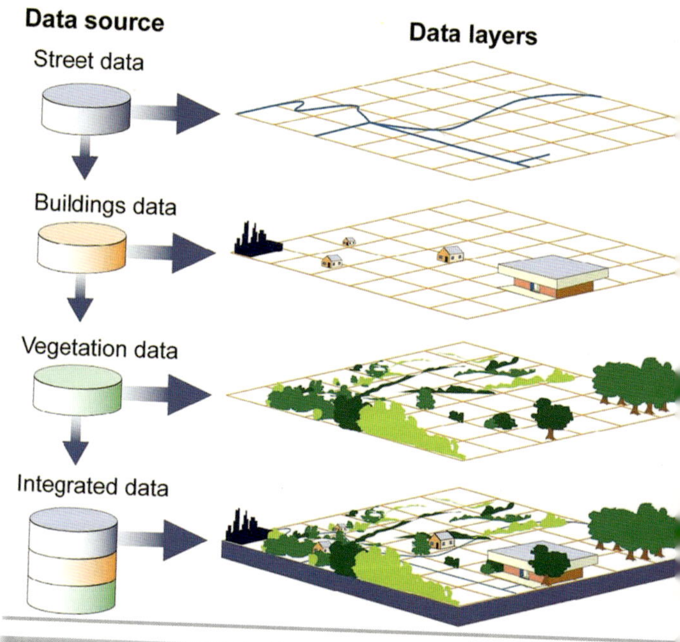

This diagram shows how a GIS brings together separate layers of data to create a single combined map.

The GIS converts the data into a standardized, or regular, format. It adjusts existing maps and satellite images so that they all have the same scale, or relative size. It uses information about different subjects to make separate layers of a map. One layer might show natural features such as wetlands, for example. Another layer might show the location of factories, places where crimes have been committed, or areas where schools are overcrowded.

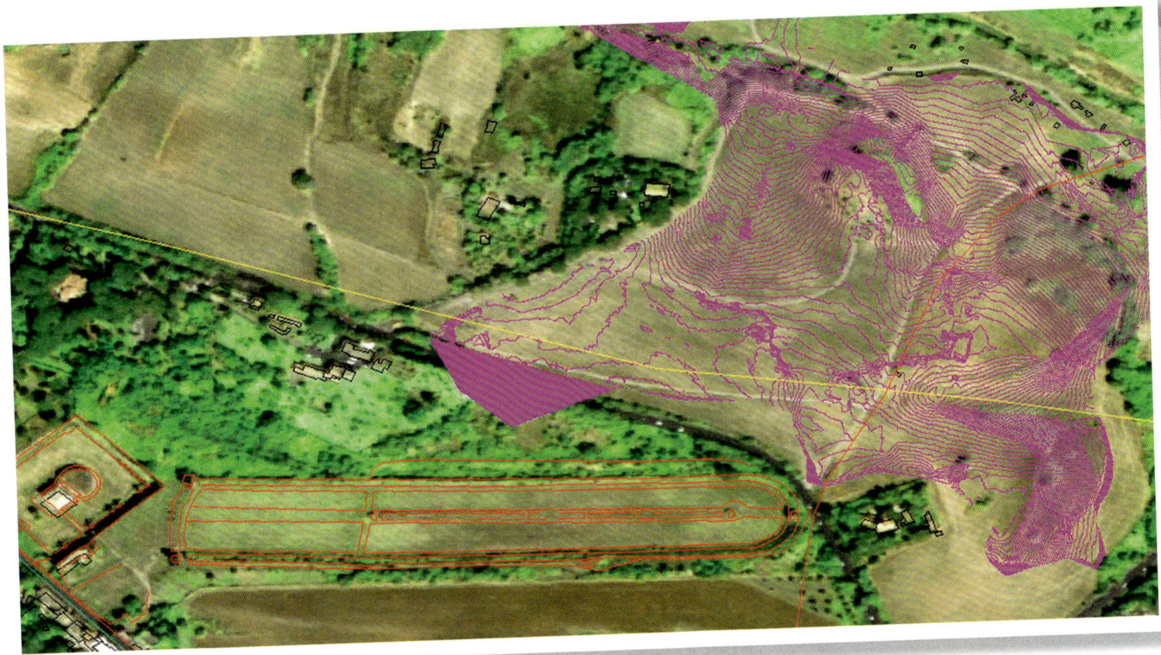

This GIS map of a park in Rome, Italy, combines a satellite image with details of the land contours (purple) and ancient underground ruins (red), including a Roman racetrack.

The data can relate to the natural world or to human activity—or both. The only requirement is that the data includes geographical information, such as a ZIP code or map coordinates. These coordinates are based on an imaginary grid of lines that covers Earth's surface. They include a position on Earth's surface from north-south (latitude), represented by horiztonal lines, and a position from east-west (longitude), represented by vertical lines.

Comparing Information

When a cartographer has gathered the information, he or she selects which layers to show on a map. It is possible to display multiple layers on the same map, and to add or remove layers easily. This makes GIS maps useful for comparing information that may have come from different sources. The same map of a neighborhood can show crime rates and the average income of the population. Or a map could show land use in Asia and the territories of threatened species such as tigers, to show where farming might damage tigers' habitats.

Did You Know?

The first GIS was introduced in 1960 by the Department of Forestry and Rural Development in Canada. The technology was improved later in the 1960s by the Laboratory for Computer Graphics and Spatial Analysis at Harvard University.

A resident uses GIS software to create a map of his neighborhood in Miami, Florida.

GIS for Individuals

The technology behind GIS is flexible, and allows data from different maps and other sources to be brought together. It also allows users to make their own maps by selecting only those layers of information they wish to include. The GIS automatically displays data from different sources at the same scale and on the same **projection**.

GIS is already affecting the lives of individuals. Some cities use GIS systems to allow residents to look up maps of their neighborhoods. These maps can show their property lines, for example, or the locations of drains or underground cables. That helps residents dig or build on their property without damaging undergound systems or building outside their property line.

GIS at Home

GIS software is widely available for home computers. This makes it increasingly easy for individuals to create their own personalized maps. In this way, digital technology is helping to take cartography out of the hands of the governments and big corporations who used to be the only people who could control maps. Soon, anyone will be able to use data to generate their own maps.

In the Real World

Local Government

Major users of GIS mapping include city halls and town halls. Some councils allow residents to access GIS maps to find out information about where they live. This could be where their local library is or where city boundaries lie. GIS can link many different sorts of information to the same point on the map. When users click that point, they are able to access all information related to their property in one visit.

Governments are creating online maps that users can change to display whatever data they require. This one shows major highways.

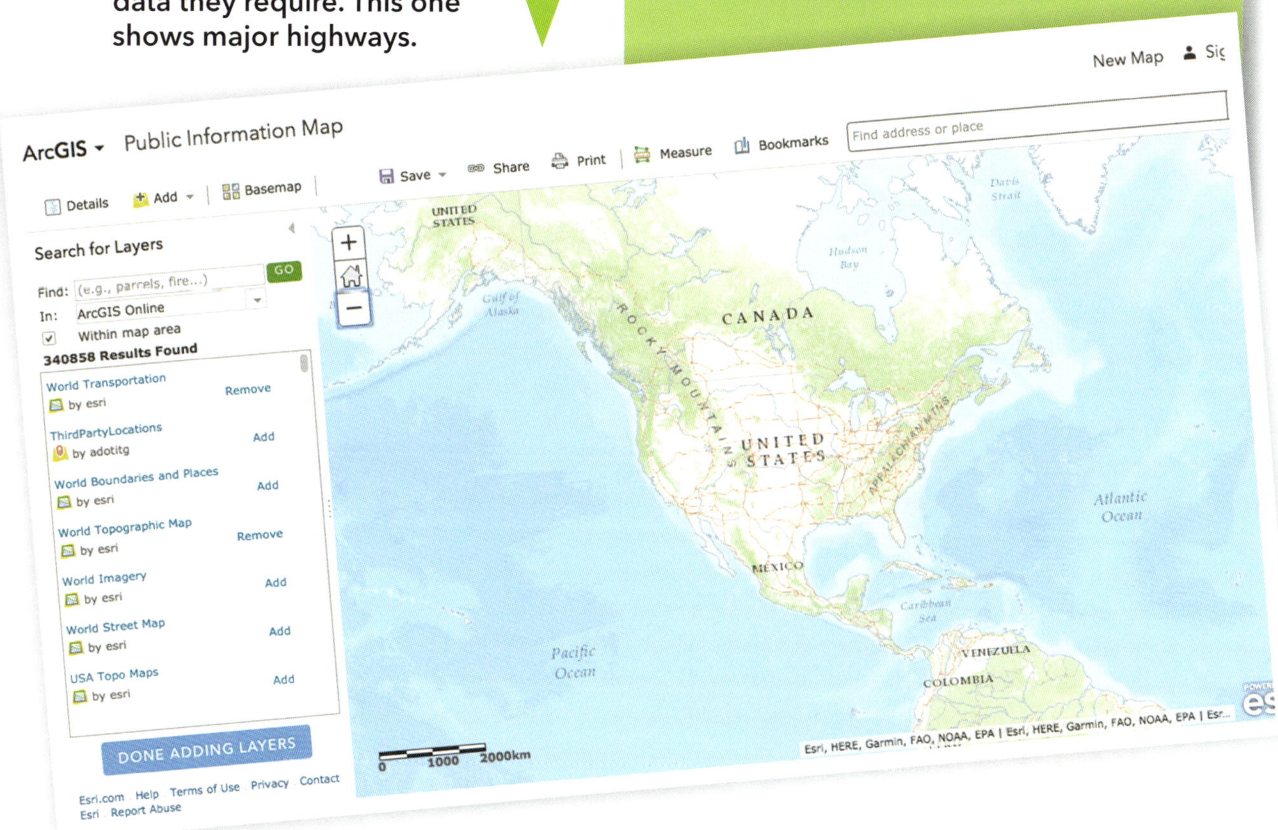

GOOGLE EARTH

For over a decade, the technology company Google has been involved in a project to map the whole planet, from entire continents down to individual streets.

The development of digital mapping technology, and improvements in cameras and computers, have encouraged the creation of the world's most ambitious cartographic project. With the latest digital technology, Google plans to create a virtual map of the entire planet–and beyond.

Google released Google Maps in 2005. The program quickly became popular as a way to get good directions for travel, real-time information on traffic problems on the way, and attractions and amenities, such as restaurants, near a destination. Google gathered street maps across the world on a single website.

Google Street View allows users to take a virtual walk through the streets of most towns and cities around the world.

Breakthroughs

Google Mars

Google's virtual mapping ambitions do not stop at Earth. The company has also set up Google Moon and Google Mars. The projects bring together maps, satellite images, and data about the Moon and Mars, including live **panoramic** images taken by NASA's Mars Exploration Rover missions.

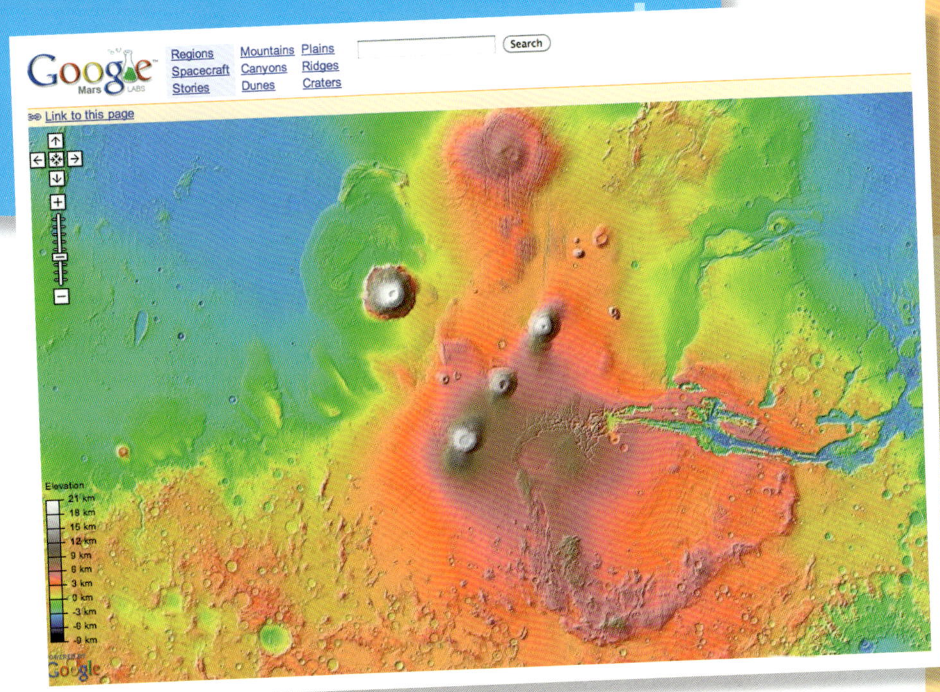

This screenshot shows a view of Google Mars. Users can change the elevation, direction, and type of map they want to see, such as maps of physical features or of the planet's geology.

It also combined street maps with satellite images to create **hybrid** views. These views showed people what neighborhoods, cities, and whole countries looked like from above.

A View of the Streets

In 2007, Google introduced Google Street View. The company used cars with special cameras on their roofs to take panoramic pictures at street level as the cars drove around. The images allowed users to pay virtual visits to cities all over the world. While Google Street View was popular, it was also controversial. People complained that it was an invasion of their privacy. Some images showed individuals or the insides of their homes. The images were posted online for anyone to see.

Google Earth

Both Google Maps and Google Street View are part of Google Earth. Google Earth began at around the same time as Google Maps, when Google purchased a GIS program called EarthViewer from a company originally funded by the Central Intelligence Agency (CIA). The program took satellite imagery, aerial photographs, and GIS information and merged it into a virtual globe. Users could zoom in and look at 3-D maps of every place on Earth. Google built on the original program. It added Street View images and building plans in order to create 3-D models of real cities such as New York, London, and Toronto. People could even fly from one place to another using a flight simulator program.

Google claims that its ambition is to put detailed maps of the whole globe into the hands of users all around the world.

For and Against

Google has made Google Earth available for free. The company wants anyone to be able to create their own maps based on information they have gathered. The software has helped

Maps and Me

Mapping Your Life

Go to Google Maps and look up your address. Explore your neighborhood using Map View, Street View, and Hybrid View. How does each view differ from the others? What would each map view be most useful for? Write down the five most important places in your daily life, such as your home and your school. Draw your own map of these locations. What type of Google Maps view would be best to display your map?

governments, students, and experts study the changing environment. Some people say that, by showing how the planet is all connected, Google Earth is a force for global well-being. They claim that it helps to reinforce the idea that we all share the same planet and are all responsible for its care. However, Google Earth has been criticized too. For example, the maps hide sensitive locations such as military bases, as requested by the government. Some people think that everyone should be able to see the maps without **censorship**.

Maps and Me

Google Earth Errors

Google Earth creates its images by combining satellite and airplane photography with 3-D models of terrain. Sometimes the process goes wrong. The angle from which the image was taken and the depth of the natural landscape do not match up, so part of the image is distorted—such as the one below. Often, human-made structures such as roads and bridges do not show up correctly. The glitches are fixed as Google updates its mapping data, but many people try to collect the fleeting images while they still exist.

The artist Clement Valla has published a collection of errors under the title *Postcards from Google Earth*.

MAPS IN YOUR WORLD

Digital technology has revolutionized maps. What sort of digital maps do you come across every day, and how do they help shape the way you see the world?

Computers and the Internet give cartographers access to huge amounts of data that they can use to generate digital maps. Digital maps come in a range of formats, from those based on satellite photographs to those that layer information on street maps, those that show change over time, and those that model landscapes in 3-D.

The maps on these pages were all created using digital technology, but they all have different purposes and use different methods for presenting data. If you were mapping your neighborhood, what different methods could you use to show what it is like today—and how it might change in the future?

This map uses color coding to show wind speeds in the United States. Rather than trying to show precise wind speeds, it uses data to produce a yearly average, from the fastest winds (blues and purples) to the lightest winds (greens). Maps like these are helpful when showing environmental trends and changes.

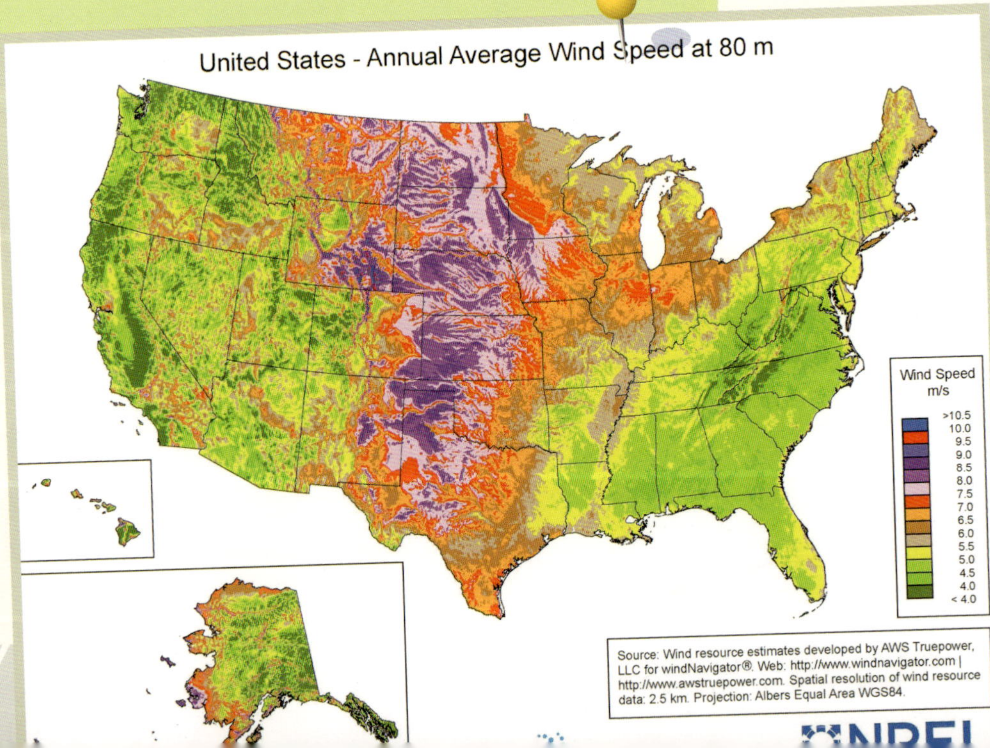

This map (left) shows the expansion of Cancun in Mexico between 1979 (left) and 2009 (right). During the 30-year period, the small fishing town grew to become a major tourist resort city.

These two city maps show Auckland, in New Zealand (right), and London, England (below). The Auckland map is intended for drivers. It is constantly updated using satellite data about traffic movement and roadworks. The London map shows the city's main streets, highways, and railroads. It uses technology from the video game Minecraft to create a semi-realistic aerial view of the city.

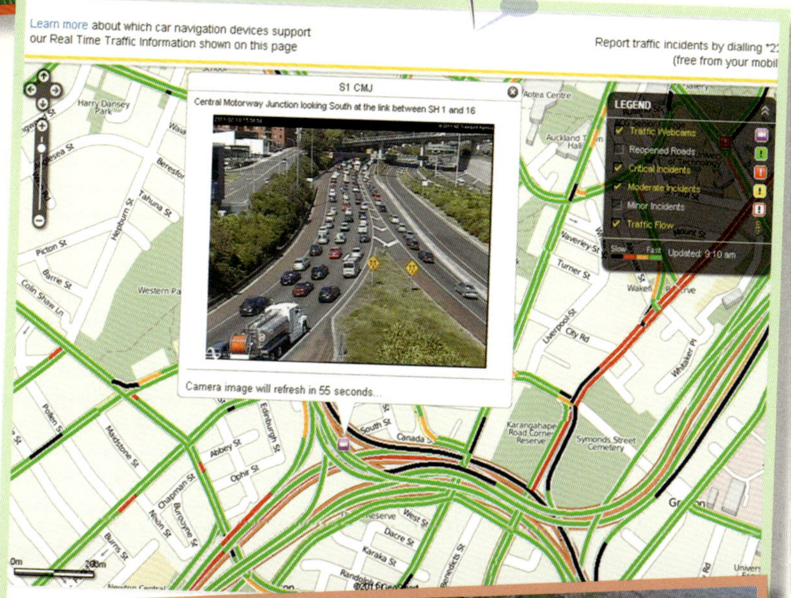

Glossary

abstract Describes something that does not have a physical existence

amateur Describes someone who does something for enjoyment rather than as a job

animation The rapid display of a sequence of still images to create a moving image, often used in cartoons

anonymize To make sure computer data cannot be linked to individuals

cartogram A map that distorts geography to convey information

cartographers People who make maps

censorship Actions by the government to prevent the spread of information

climate change The long-term change in Earth's climate caused by human activity

contour lines Lines on a map that join places of the same height above sea level

customized Tailored to a specific user

data Information and statistics

database A large collection of data stored in a way that is easy to access

deforestation The process of cutting down forest trees on a large scale

digital Stored in binary code and displayed on computers

fictional Existing only in the imagination

fractals In geometry, shapes that are made up by the repetition of identical smaller shapes

Geographic Information Systems (GIS) Computer programs that use a wide range of sources to generate maps

geology The make-up of rocks in Earth's surface

Global Positioning System (GPS) A system of satellites used to provide accurate locations on Earth

hybrid Describes an image that combines a map with a satellite photograph

ice cap A large covering of ice at either of Earth's poles

infrared A type of light that is not visible to the human eye

key A system of coloring or symbols used to convey information on a map

location services Software that uses a user's location to tailor features on their smartphone or tablet

meteorologists People who study and predict the weather

models Computer programs that use past events to predict future events

mosaic A picture created by putting together smaller pieces

ocean currents Large, moving streams of water that move through the oceans

panoramic Having a wide view

pixel A single dot of illumination in an image on a display screen

projection The way in which a map creates a flat image of a spherical object

relief The differences of height in a landscape

simulation A realistic computer re-creation of a real experience

topographic Relating to the physical features of an area

virtual Describes something that does not exist but that is made to appear real by a computer

On the Web

earth.google.com
Google Earth allows you to explore the whole planet. Look up satellite photos and maps, see buildings in 3-D, and explore canyons on the seabed.

www.animaps.com
This site gives users the ability to create dynamic, moving maps using information from Google Maps. The site includes a tutorial for new users.

http://mapmaker.nationalgeographic.org
This National Geographic site allows users to customize base maps with layers of different information.

http://hint.fm/wind/
This site allows you to look at the latest video maps of winds blowing in the United States.

Books

Gray, Leon. *How Does GPS Work?* (High-Tech Science). Gareth Stevens, 2014.

Matteson, Adrienne. *Using Digital Maps* (Information Explorer). Cherry Lake Publishing, 2013.

Mizielinska, Aleksandra, and Daniel Mizielinski. *Maps*. Big Picture, 2013.

Panchyk, Richard. *Charting the World: Geography and Maps from Cave Paintings to GPS with 21 Activities.* Chicago Review, 2011.

Quinlan, Julia J. *GPS and Computer Maps* (How to Use Maps). PowerKids Press, 2012.

Index